# Sacraments and Social Mission

## LIVING THE GOSPEL, BEING DISCIPLES

**Department of Justice, Peace and Human Development**

United States Conference of Catholic Bishops
Washington, DC

Photos: Dreamstime, Bigstock, Fotolia, and Shutterstock

First printing, January 2013
Second printing, February 2015
ISBN 978-1-60137-349-6

# CONTENTS

# INTRODUCTION

In *Deus Caritas Est* (*God Is Love*), Pope Benedict XVI writes that "love for widows and orphans, prisoners, and the sick and needy of every kind, is as essential to [the Church] as the ministry of the sacraments and preaching of the Gospel" (no. 22). Proclaiming the Word of God, celebrating the sacraments, and exercising the ministry of charity, he says, are "inseparable" (no. 25). In other words, there is an essential connection between our faith and the way we put love into action in the world.

This guide is for priests and lay ministers, teachers and students, adults and young people, and those who are preparing for the sacraments. It is for all Catholics who seek to better understand the connections between the celebration of the sacraments and our social mission as followers of Jesus and members of the Body of Christ.

# HANDOUTS

All of the handouts included in this book can be downloaded and duplicated. Visit "Resources and Tools" at **www.usccb.org/jphd.**

# HOW TO USE THIS RESOURCE

Here are some ideas for how you can use this resource with a variety of audiences and in many settings.

## Priests and Deacons

Help parishioners better understand the richness of the sacraments and the call to live our faith and carry out our gospel mission in the world. Make these connections while celebrating Baptisms and marriages, in homilies, in bulletins, and through efforts to prepare parishioners for the sacraments.

## Religious Education

Strengthen lesson plans by integrating the handouts, prayers, and discussion questions, or use the session outline for a stand-alone lesson for growing in discipleship through the sacraments.

## Adult Faith Formation

Use these resources to offer formation and programs for adults to learn, reflect, and discuss as we all strive to follow Christ, strengthened by the sacraments. Consider offering a program for parents while children meet for religious education programming.

## Sacramental Preparation

Religion teachers and religious educators, RCIA coordinators and sponsors, and others can help those preparing for the sacraments to reflect prayerfully on the social dimensions of the sacraments and the call to discipleship. For example:

- **Baptism:** Deepen parents' understanding of their child's— and their own—Baptism. Integrate materials into RCIA programming.
- **Confirmation:** Help Confirmation candidates understand their call to be disciples and carry on Christ's mission in the world.
- **Eucharist:** Help those preparing for their First Eucharist to reflect on the social dimensions of Eucharist and the call to Eucharistic living.
- **Penance and Reconciliation:** Use the handout to teach about social dimensions of sin. The questions on the back of the handout can help penitents examine their consciences.
- **Anointing of the Sick:** Deepen the experience of those who minister to the sick, and help those who are ill and their families be witnesses to others.
- **Marriage:** Reflect with engaged couples during individual meetings, or include content on the social responsibilities of marriage as part of pre-Cana programming.

- **Holy Orders:** Help those preparing to be priests imitate Christ's mission of service and justice.

## Small Faith Sharing Communities

Use the session outline at the end of this resource to deepen understanding of a different sacrament each week, for seven or eight weeks, and grow in love of God and neighbor.

## Families

Use the handouts or the session outline as a basis for dinner conversation and family discussion.

## Youth Ministry Programs

Help young people to reflect on their faith and baptismal call, deepen their understanding of the Eucharist, experience Confirmation as a call to discipleship, and engage in more meaningful examination of consciences during Penance and Reconciliation.

## Advent and Lent

Use the Penance and Reconciliation handout as a tool for reflection in preparation for communal Penance services during Advent and Lent, and for individuals preparing for confession. During Lent, use the session outlines to offer a structured program for parishioners to reflect on the meaning of the Sacraments of Initiation that will be celebrated on Easter.

## Seminary Rectors and Directors of Priestly Formation

Integrate these materials into courses and formation on the sacraments, liturgy, moral theology, and others, as well as pastoral training, placements, and reflection.

## Extraordinary Ministers, Chaplains, Caretakers, and Persons Who Are Ill

Use the Eucharist and Anointing of the Sick handouts to reflect on the social dimensions of these sacraments, the meaning of the Body of Christ, the Church's mission of healing and compassion, and the service and witness of those who are ill.

## Prayer Before the Blessed Sacrament

Provide the Eucharist handout as a reflection tool for those praying before the Blessed Sacrament.

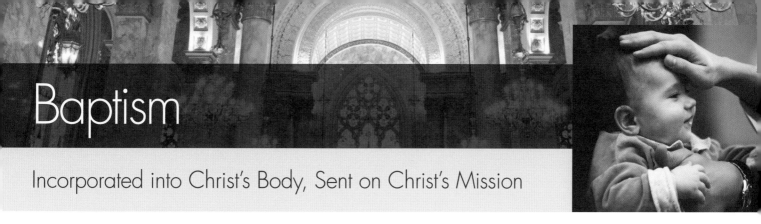

# Baptism

## Incorporated into Christ's Body, Sent on Christ's Mission

The sacraments celebrated by the Church are signs of grace that make a deeper reality present to us. One reality we encounter through the sacraments is Christ's presence in the Church community, his Body. This recognition of Christ's presence in the community should lead to a stronger awareness of being sent on mission to engage in love-inspired action in the world.

As Pope Benedict XVI notes in *Deus Caritas Est* (*God Is Love*), the celebration of the sacraments and the ministry of love are "inseparable." Love in action, he says, is "an indispensable expression" of the Church's being (no. 25).

This guide focuses on the Sacrament of Baptism, the rite of initiation into the Christian community. As you read, consider the meaning of your own Baptism, your membership in the community, and the mission on which you are sent.

## Baptism makes us "members of one another."

Since the time of early Christianity, Baptism has been the rite of initiation into the Christian community of the Church. In Baptism, the "one Spirit" makes us members of the Body of Christ and of "one another" (*Catechism of the Catholic Church* [CCC], no. 1267). Pope John Paul II describes the result of Baptism as a "mystical unity" between Christ and his disciples, and the disciples with one another, like "branches of a single vine." This reflects the mystical communion of the Holy Trinity (*Christifideles Laici* [*The Vocation and the Mission of the Lay Faithful in the Church and in the World*], no. 12).

## Baptism reveals the equality and dignity of each member of the community.

In the one Body of Christ, all the members share "a common dignity" so that "no inequality arising from race or nationality, social condition or sex" exists, for all are one in Christ (*Lumen Gentium* [*Dogmatic Constitution on the Church*], no. 32).

## Baptism requires us to reject sin and re-assess our values, decisions, and lifestyles.

During the Rite of Baptism, we reject sin, renouncing those beliefs, values, and choices that are opposed to Christ. We also reject sinful attitudes that degrade the dignity of others (e.g., racism, sexism, etc.) and practices that prevent other members of our human family from living in dignity (e.g., abortion, policies that hurt the poor, etc.). Baptism calls us to reject death and embrace life and dignity for all.

## In Baptism, we profess our commitment to the Church's beliefs, values, and vision.

At Baptism, we embrace a unique vision and set of values: those of the community of the Church, whose values prioritize love for God, self, others, and all of creation. The rest of the community also joins in the profession of faith, illustrating that the community is linked across generations, space, and time.

## Baptism invites us to a vocation of holiness and the practice of charity.

In Baptism, we receive a "vocation to holiness," which is "intimately connected" to our membership in the "Communion of Saints," which strives to make present the "Kingdom of God in history." Participation in the Communion of Saints requires a commitment to communion with Christ and "a life of charity" in "this world and in the next" (*Christifideles Laici*, nos. 17, 19).

## Baptism incorporates us into the life, Death, and Resurrection of Christ and the ongoing work of the Holy Spirit in the world.

The *Compendium of the Social Doctrine of the Church* (*Compendium*) reminds us, "By Baptism, the laity are incorporated into Christ and are made participants in his life and mission" (no. 541). The triple immersion in the baptismal water signifies the death of sin and entry into the newness of life through Christ's Death and Resurrection. The oil signifies anointing by the Holy Spirit and receiving of the Holy Spirit's gifts. The Holy Spirit helps us to imitate Jesus' self-sacrificial love and allows us to share in the work of the Holy Spirit in the world.

## Baptism leads us to imitate Christ's example.

The baptized are called to imitate Jesus' example and strive in thought, word, and action to live his love. This means working to heal the wounds of sin, living the Beatitudes, practicing the twofold commandment of love of God and neighbor, and imitating the lives of the saints (CCC, nos. 1694-97). Having been anointed by the Spirit, "Christians can repeat in an individual way the words of Jesus: 'The Spirit of the Lord is upon me, because he has anointed me to preach good news to the poor. He has sent me to proclaim release to captives and recovering of sight to the blind, to set at liberty those who are oppressed, to proclaim the acceptable year of the Lord' . . . (Lk 4:18-19)" (*Christifideles Laici*, no. 13).

## Baptism makes us disciples to the world.

Incorporation into Christ and into the community of the People of God means agreeing to take part in, and to self-identify with, its mission to become disciples in the world (CCC, no. 1276, and *Compendium*, no. 541). Pope John Paul II writes, "Because of the one dignity flowing from Baptism," every baptized person "shares a responsibility for the Church's mission" (*Christifideles Laici*, no. 15). The baptized must work as disciples of Christ by caring for the sick, the oppressed, the debilitated, and the sinners. We are called to carry out this work not only in our local communities, but also in the global community of which we are also members. In this way, we can extend to all the love, compassion, and mercy of God that we ourselves have come to know.

## Baptism calls us to live in the world, seeking the Kingdom in our daily lives.

During the blessing of the baptismal waters at the Easter Vigil, we recall God's action within history. We hear, for example, about the liberation of Israel from slavery in Egypt. Christians believe that "Baptism does not take [the baptized] from the world at all." Instead, the world becomes the "place" and "means" for the lay faithful to "fulfill their Christian vocation" (*Christifideles Laici*, no. 15). We give expression to our baptismal reality "in our daily lives" in "the field" of the world (Pope Benedict XVI, *Sacramentum Caritatis*

[*Sacrament of Charity*], no. 79). The baptized work within the spheres of "work, culture, science and research; the exercise of social, economic and political responsibilities" to order them to the Kingdom (*Compendium*, no. 543).

The baptized are called to contribute to the sanctification of the world. Being "present and active in the world" is a "theological and ecclesiological reality" (*Compendium*, no. 543). This reality is what leads us to work to protect the life and dignity of all people and to care for God's creation here on earth. "The world is not something indifferent, raw material to be utilized simply as we see fit," Pope Benedict XVI, notes. Instead, we see it as "God's creation." Our Baptism helps us see a "profound relationship" between our work here on earth and our future with Christ (*Sacramentum Caritatis*, no. 92).

## The baptized are to live as lights in the darkness.

After being baptized, we acknowledge or receive a white garment to signify that we have risen with Christ. We receive a lighted candle, which symbolizes that we are a new creation, enlightened by Christ. We are now called to carry that light into the dark world to extend the light to others (CCC, no. 1243). The gifts given at Baptism, Pope Benedict XVI writes, are for "the building up of Christ's Body (1 Cor 12) and for ever greater witness to the Gospel in the world" (*Sacramentum Caritatis*, no. 17).

QUESTION FOR REFLECTION

What is the connection between your Baptism and work to protect the life and dignity of every person?

# Confirmation

## Strengthened by the Spirit, Called to Action

Confirmation enriches the baptized with the strength of the Holy Spirit so that they can better witness to Christ in word and deed (*Catechism of the Catholic Church* [CCC], no. 1285). Anointed by the Holy Spirit at Confirmation, Christians strengthen their bond with the Church and become better equipped to carry out the Church's mission of love and service.

### At Confirmation, our faith and membership in the Body of Christ is confirmed, or strengthened.

In the Rite of Baptism, we become new members of the Body of Christ, but our journey does not end there. The decision to be baptized is followed by continued growth, learning, and witness as members of the Body of Christ. Our desire to continue to grow and develop as Christians finds expression in Confirmation, when we renew our baptismal promises and receive in a new way the gift of the Holy Spirit, which strengthens our "bond" with the Church and its members (CCC, no. 1316, and Pope John Paul II, *Redemptoris Missio* [*On the Permanent Validity of the Church's Missionary Mandate*], no. 26).

### Confirmation connects us to a larger community.

The relationship of the bishop (who presides over the Rite of Confirmation) with the church community in a given area reminds us of our connection to the larger community of the Church, which is global. Thus, Confirmation reminds us that we belong to the Universal Church and to a local parish community (CCC, no. 1309). The sacred Chrism oil used during Confirmation points to the community's sharing of the Spirit, since the same oil is used during Baptism and to anoint bishops and priests during the Sacrament of Holy Orders. Oil for the Anointing of the Sick is also consecrated during Holy Week. The symbol of oil reminds us of the action of the Holy Spirit upon us as members in the Church family.

### At Confirmation, we receive the gifts of the Holy Spirit.

In the Gospels, the same Spirit that descended on Jesus during Baptism descends on the Apostles at Pentecost (CCC, nos. 1285-1287). The readings and homily we hear at Confirmation remind us that this same Spirit is present to us today. At Confirmation, we receive diverse spiritual gifts that work together for the "common good" and "the building up of the Church, to the well-being of humanity and to the needs of the world" (Pope John Paul II, *Christifideles Laici* [*The Vocation and the Mission of the Lay Faithful in the Church and in the World*], no. 24). At Confirmation, we pray for an increase of the gifts of the Spirit in our own lives in order to serve the cause of justice and peace in Church and world.

### The Spirit moves us to imitate the love and service of Christ and the saints.

In preparation for the Sacrament of Confirmation, we often perform many hours of service to help those in need. In doing so, we practice love and service in imitation of the saints whose names we often take at Confirmation. Anointed at Confirmation, we are further strengthened to live lives that give off "the aroma of Christ" as did the holy saints (CCC, no. 1294). The sacred Chrism is mixed with fragrant spices precisely to symbolize this "aroma."

The Holy Spirit pours love into our hearts so that we can become "instruments of grace" in order to "pour forth God's charity and to weave networks of charity" in the world (Pope Benedict XVI, *Caritas in Veritate*

[*Charity in Truth*], no. 5). The Holy Spirit "harmonizes" our hearts with Christ's heart and moves us to love others as Christ loved when he washed the disciples' feet and gave his life for us (Pope Benedict XVI, *Deus Caritas Est* [*God Is Love*], no. 19).

## At Confirmation, we recommit to participate in the Church's work and mission.

Sealing with the gift of the Spirit at Confirmation strengthens us for ongoing service in the Body of Christ in the Church and in the world. It prepares us to be active participants in the Church's mission and to "bear witness to the Christian faith in words accompanied by deeds" (CCC, no. 1316). Finally, the Spirit sends us as workers in the vineyard and instruments of the Holy Spirit in renewing the earth and promoting God's Kingdom of justice and peace.

Thus, Confirmation is not only an *anointing*, but also a *commissioning* to live out our faith *in the world*. We are already called to mission by virtue of our Baptism, but at Confirmation we are endowed with gifts of the Spirit (like the Apostles in Acts 2) to be "ever greater witness[es] to the Gospel in the world" (Pope Benedict XVI, *Sacramentum Caritatis* [*Sacrament of Charity*], no. 17). As disciples and witnesses to Christ in both Church and world (CCC, no. 1319), we are sent out to act on behalf of the poor and vulnerable, promoting the life and dignity of every human person.

## The Holy Spirit inspires us to Gospel action that includes human development and work to end injustice.

The Holy Spirit inspires the work of evangelization, which includes work not only for all peoples' spiritual well-being, but also the evangelization of systems and cultures (Pope John Paul II, *Redemptoris Missio*, nos. 42, 65). The Church's missionary activity includes a "commitment to peace, development and the liberation of peoples; the rights of individuals and peoples, especially those of minorities; the advancement of women and children; safeguarding the created world," and many other areas of action in the world (*Redemptoris Missio*, no. 37).

In addition, action inspired by the Holy Spirit calls us to "bear witness to Christ by taking courageous and prophetic stands in the face of the corruption of political or economic power." The Spirit also "overcomes barriers and divisions of race, caste, or ideology" and makes the Christian-on-mission into "a sign of God's love in the world—a love without exclusion or partiality" (*Redemptoris Missio*, nos. 43, 89).

## Confirmation calls us to share Christ's mission to promote life and dignity.

The baptized, anointed by the Holy Spirit, are incorporated into Christ, who is priest, prophet, and king, and called to share in his mission (CCC, no. 1241). We share Christ's **priestly** mission by giving of ourselves daily in union with Christ's supreme sacrifice on the Cross. As **prophets**, we announce the Kingdom of God in both word and deed and we witness to the Gospel in family, social life, and community, and in our commitment to human life and dignity. We share the **kingly** mission by seeking God's Kingdom of justice in the world. We do this when we overcome the kingdom of sin, give of ourselves, recognize Jesus in "the least of these" (cf. Mt 25:40), and work for justice and peace.

All those anointed by the Spirit at Baptism and Confirmation share Christ's mission in Luke 4:18-19: "The Spirit of the Lord is upon me, / because he has anointed me / to bring glad tidings to the poor. / He has sent me to proclaim liberty to captives / and recovery of sight to the blind, / to let the oppressed go free, / and to proclaim a year acceptable to the Lord" (see also *Christifideles Laici*, nos. 13-14).

## QUESTIONS FOR REFLECTION

- *Membership in the community.* What does it mean to be part of the Body of Christ?
- *Gifts of the Spirit.* What gifts have you been given? How are you called to use those gifts to benefit others?
- *Listening to God's call.* Who are you called to be? What are you called to do with your life?

- *Mission in the world.* What is the mission of the Church? What is your role in carrying it out? To what are you com*missioned*?
- *The witness of the saints.* How do the lives of the saints inspire you to "give off the aroma of Christ"?

# Eucharist

## Body of Christ, Broken for the World

The Eucharist is "the source and summit of the Christian life" (*Lumen Gentium* [*Dogmatic Constitution on the Church*], no. 11). In the Eucharistic Liturgy and our prayer before the Blessed Sacrament, we encounter God's presence in personal and profound ways. But the Eucharist is also social, as Pope Benedict XVI reminds us in *Deus Caritas Est* (*God Is Love*): "A Eucharist which does not pass over into the concrete practice of love is intrinsically fragmented" (no. 14). The Eucharist, celebrated as a community, teaches us about human dignity, calls us to right relationship with God, ourselves, and others. As the Body of Christ, it sends us on mission to help transform our communities, neighborhoods, and world. Church teaching, rooted in both Scripture and Tradition, emphasizes both the personal and social natures of the Eucharist. This guide highlights Popes Paul VI, John Paul II, and Benedict XVI's writings about the social nature of the Eucharist. Their words challenge and move us to encounter Christ in the Eucharist in ways both personal and social.

## We experience the Eucharist as a community.

The Eucharist draws each of us closer to Christ as individuals, but also as a community. As Catholics, we never really worship alone. At the Eucharistic Liturgy, we gather with the young and old, the rich and poor, as well as millions around the world and the saints in heaven, to celebrate Christ's sacrifice. This powerful reality reminds us, in the words of Pope John Paul II: "A truly Eucharistic community cannot be closed in upon itself", (*Ecclesia de Eucharistia* [*On the Eucharist*], no. 39); rather the Eucharist challenges us to recognize our place within a community and the human family.

## The Eucharist awakens us to our own dignity and to that of others.

The Eucharist is a sign of our incomparable dignity as human persons. This dignity, given to all equally, regardless of our social or economic status or where we come from (Jas 2:1-9), causes us to recognize "what value each person, our brother or sister, has in God's eyes, if Christ offers Himself equally to each one. . . . If our Eucharistic worship is authentic, it must make us grow in awareness of the dignity of each person," Pope John Paul II writes (*Dominicae Cenae* [*On the Mystery and Worship of the Eucharist*], no. 6).

## The Eucharist unifies and heals divisions.

St. Paul taught that the celebration of the Eucharist is insincere if there are divisions within the community based on class (1 Cor 11), status, or privilege (Rom 12), or if there are factions within the community (1 Cor 1). Partaking in the Sacrament as equals in the Body of Christ challenges us to unity as one family.

## The Eucharist sensitizes us to those who suffer.

As we meditate on the Eucharist, we experience Christ's love for us—and for others. In the depth of prayer, we become so moved and sensitized to his love for those who suffer that the words of St. Augustine become a reality for us: "The pain of one, even the smallest member, is the pain of all" (*Sermo Denis*).

## The Eucharist moves us and inspires us to respond.

In the Eucharist, the boundlessness of the Father's love "springs up within us a lively response" that causes us to "begin to love" (*Dominicae Cenae*, no. 5). Contemplating Christ's sacrifice for the world in need, we are compelled to follow his example. Drawn "into the very dynamic of his self-giving" we are moved to self-giving action in solidarity with the members of our human family who face injustice (*Deus Caritas Est*, no. 13). St. John Chrysostom's words in the fourth century become real for us as we reflect on Matthew 25:31-46: Do you wish to honor the Body of Christ? Do not ignore him when he is naked.

## Eucharist-inspired love allows us to live out our Christian vocation.

Pope John Paul II writes that our ability to go and do likewise in imitation of Jesus' washing of the disciples' feet is the "criterion by which the authenticity of our Eucharistic celebrations is judged" (*Mane Nobiscum Domine* [*Stay with us, Lord*], no. 28). "Eucharistic worship," he says, is the expression of "the love that springs up within us from the Eucharist"—that love which is "the authentic and deepest characteristic of the Christian vocation" (*Dominicae Cenae*, no. 5).

## The Eucharist challenges us to recognize and confront structures of sin.

The Risen Christ in the Eucharist acts as "a compelling force for inner renewal, an inspiration to change the structures of sin in which individuals, communities and at times entire peoples are entangled" (Pope John Paul II, *Dies Domini* [*On Keeping the Lord's Day Holy*], no. 73). These structures include racism, violence, injustice, poverty, exploitation, and all other systemic degradation of human life or dignity. As Pope Benedict XVI reminds us, our "fraternal communion" in the Eucharist leads to "a determination to transform unjust structures and to restore respect for the dignity of all men and women, created in God's image and likeness" (Pope Benedict XVI, *Sacramentum Caritatis* [*Sacrament of Charity*], no. 89).

## The Eucharist prepares us for mission.

In the face of the sin and injustice we see present in our communities and in our world, the Eucharist "plants a seed of living hope in our daily commitment to the work before us," challenging us to live "Eucharistic" lives. It affirms our role as citizens and as men and women in various professions at different levels of society in "contributing with the light of the Gospel to the building of a more human world, a world fully in harmony with God's plan" (*Ecclesia de Eucharistia*, no. 20).

## The Eucharist propels us forth to transform the world.

The Eucharist "increases, rather than lessens, *our sense of responsibility for the world* today." Christ in the Eucharist calls us to build "a more human world, a world fully in harmony with God's plan" (*Ecclesia de Eucharistia*, no. 20). Filled with awe for all we have received in Christ's self-gift, we respond with service and works of charity. We act to transform unjust structures, policies, and laws that degrade human life and dignity.

## QUESTIONS FOR PRAYER AND REFLECTION BEFORE THE EUCHARIST

1. Spend some time reflecting on the passages from papal writings that are included in this handout.
   - Which do you find inspiring?
   - Which do you find challenging?
   - How might God be speaking to you?
2. What issues affecting your community and the world today weigh deeply on your heart? Spend some time bringing these concerns before the Blessed Sacrament.
3. During your time before Christ in the Eucharist, can you sense his compassion? Love? Desire to transform all that opposes human life and dignity?
4. What gifts has God, the Father, given you? How might he be asking you to use these gifts in the service of others?
5. How does the Eucharistic meal compel you to care for those who are hungry?
6. How might the Holy Spirit be moving you to join with others to respond to problems in your family, neighborhood, or community?

# The Eucharistic Liturgy

## Formed, Transformed, and Sent

The Eucharist is the "sign" and "cause" of our communion with God and our unity as the People of God. In the Eucharist, we "unite ourselves with the heavenly liturgy" and with one another. Together transformed, we are then sent forth to fulfill God's will in our daily lives (*Catechism of the Catholic Church* [CCC], nos. 1325-26, 1332). In this way, the Eucharistic Liturgy is social in nature. It is the celebration through which God draws us into communion with himself and with others, forming and transforming us to live as the Body of Christ in the world.

### Gathering

The gathering for worship and the Introductory Rites emphasize our coming together as a community. From our individual lives and situations, we gather as one family. At the entrance song, we raise our voices in a united chorus. The ordained minister leads us in the Sign of the Cross, which recalls the Trinity's divine communion of persons and to which we respond with one communal voice. As we make the Sign of the Cross, we turn to God, opening ourselves to his transforming presence.

### Penitential Act

During the Penitential Act, we acknowledge the sin that affects our relationship with God, ourselves, others, and the world around us. We seek Christ's healing love and forgiveness in order that we might be transformed—both as individuals and as a community, into a people of love. During the *Confiteor*, we ask the members of our heavenly community, "blessed Mary ever-Virgin, all the Angels and Saints," and our brothers and sisters around us to pray for us, and we for them.

### Liturgy of the Word

At this time, we hear a "proclamation of God's wonderful works in the history of salvation" (Pope Paul VI, *Sacrosanctum Concilium* [*Constitution on the Sacred Liturgy*], no. 35). Through the Scriptures, we also receive teaching, correction, and training in righteousness (2 Tm 3:16). We are guided and instructed in faith and in how to live in right relationship with God, others, ourselves, and creation.

### Universal Prayer or Prayer of the Faithful

As Pope John Paul II writes, "The Prayer of the Faithful responds not only to the needs of the particular Christian community but also to those of all humanity," and the Church "makes her own 'the joys and hopes, the sorrows and anxieties of people today, especially of the poor and all those who suffer'" (*Dies Domini* [*On Keeping the Lord's Day Holy*], no. 38).

### Preparation of the Gifts

Bringing forth donations to share with the poor along with the bread and the wine was part of the tradition of even the first Christian communities. The writings of SS. Paul, Ambrose, John Chrysostom, Justin Martyr, and Cyprian describe these donations for use to help orphans and widows, the sick, the imprisoned, and sojourning strangers. Pope John Paul II reminds us that we bring more than our money or donations, bread, and wine to the altar; we also bring our hearts. Through the presentation of the gifts, we contribute to "a demanding *culture of sharing*, to be lived not only among the members of the community itself but also in society as a whole" (*Dies Domini*, no. 70).

### The Eucharistic Prayer

During the Eucharistic Prayer, the priest prays that we might share in the fellowship of the apostles, saints, and martyrs—recalling real and inspiring examples of the "very many saints who are living examples for us of Eucharistic worship" (Pope John Paul II, *Dominicae Cenae* [*On the Mystery and Worship of the Eucharist*], no. 5). As the

Eucharistic Prayer continues, the reality of Christ's sacrifice is proclaimed for us in order to make us "a holy people" and to allow us to "enjoy for ever the fullness of [God's] glory." The fourth prayer reminds us of the Father's desire "that we might live no longer for ourselves" and that his Spirit would bring "to perfection his work in the world."

During the *consecration*, the Holy Spirit transforms the gifts on the altar into the Body and Blood of Jesus. Christ's sacrifice does not remain at the altar but also enters into our hearts as we participate in it, that we might come to know and model the love that is present in the sacrifice. This *memorial* (which he said to do "in memory of me") recalls Christ's words at the Last Supper. His sacrificial act strengthens our faith and also draws us to "enter into the very dynamic of his self-giving" (Pope Benedict XVI, *Deus Caritas Est* [*God Is Love*], no. 13).

## The Communion Rite

During the Lord's Prayer, we praise the Father, pray for the coming of his Kingdom on earth, and recall again our need for reconciliation to God and others. At the Rite of Peace, we extend our hands and our hearts to one another in a sign of communion and charity. We then ask the Lamb of God for mercy and peace.

Before the priest raises the host, he proclaims how Christ, through "the will of the Father and the work of the Holy Spirit" brought "life to the world." On behalf of the congregation, he prays, "Keep me always faithful to your commandments, and never let me be parted from you." In praying to be faithful to the Church's teachings, God's help is sought in our daily lives to follow the mandates of Scripture and the

tradition of our Church, which lead us to right and loving relationship with God, ourselves, and others.

Before receiving Communion, we acknowledge our unworthiness and pray for God's healing for ourselves and our community. We prepare for communion with Christ and the Spirit, but also with one another. Pope John Paul II writes in *Dominicae Cenae*, "We approach as a community the table." We receive Christ as "a gift and grace for each individual" but also "in the unity of His body which is the Church" (no. 4). The Eucharist is a "sacrament of [the Church's] unity" (no. 12).

## Final Blessing and Dismissal

The Concluding Rites with the Dismissal prepare us for mission: empowered by the Holy Spirit, we live out our baptismal consecration in the world. Renewed by the Eucharist, we are sent back into our daily lives to transform our communities and world.

Pope John Paul II writes that the Prayer after Communion, Final Blessing, and Dismissal should lead "all who have shared in the Eucharist" to "a deeper sense of the responsibility which is entrusted to them." Returning to their daily lives, Christ's disciples are called to "make their whole life a gift, a spiritual sacrifice pleasing to God (cf. Rom 12:1). They feel indebted to their brothers and sisters because of what they have received in the celebration" (*Dies Domini*, no. 45).

The Good News we have received should overflow into our lives and move us to mission in the world. Thus, the Concluding Rites are not an end but a beginning, calling us to make our entire lives "Eucharistic," so that "the Christian who takes part in the Eucharist learns

to become a *promoter of communion, peace and solidarity* in every situation" (Pope John Paul II, *Mane Nobiscum Domine* [*Stay with Us, Lord*], no. 27). Pope John Paul II issues this challenge:

Why not make the Lord's Day a more intense time of sharing, encouraging all the inventiveness of which Christian charity is capable? Inviting to a meal people who are alone, visiting the sick, providing food for needy families, spending a few hours in voluntary work and acts of solidarity: these would certainly be ways of bringing into people's lives the love of Christ received at the Eucharistic table. (*Dies Domini*, no. 72)

Likewise, Pope Benedict XVI reminds us that our "fraternal communion" in the Eucharist, must lead to "a determination to transform unjust structures and to restore respect for the dignity of all men and women, created in God's image and likeness" (Pope Benedict XVI, *Sacramentum Caritatis* [*Sacrament of Charity*], no. 89). Transformation by Christ in the Eucharist should compel us to address injustices that degrade the life or dignity of others—the poor, the unborn, immigrants, the elderly— all brothers and sisters in need.

Learn about the *Roman Missal* at **www.usccb.org/ romanmissal**.

# Penance and Reconciliation

## Reconciled to Right Relationship, Called to Heal and Restore

The new life in Christ that begins in Baptism may be weakened or lost through sin. Sin ruptures not only our relationship with God but also with our brothers and sisters.

By the nourishing light of the Holy Spirit, we are able to prepare for the Sacrament of Penance by examining our consciences to identify those ways in which we are not in right relationship with God and with others. This examination also challenges us to recognize our own participation in the "structures of sin" that degrade others' lives and dignity.

Through the Sacrament of Penance, God offers mercy and forgiveness. In response to this gift, we are called to become vehicles of Christ's love, making amends and restoring justice and the bonds that have been broken. Healed and forgiven, we are sent to work for peace, justice, and love in our communities and world.

## Sin damages our relationship with God and neighbor.

In the Gospels, Jesus teaches that love of God and love of neighbor are intimately connected (Mt 22:38-39; Mk 12:29-31). When we sin against those in need by failing to act compassionately toward them, we ignore Christ himself (Mt 25:31-46). In the words of Pope Benedict XVI, "Closing our eyes to our neighbor also blinds us to God" (*Deus Caritas Est* [*God Is Love*], no. 16). Sin ruptures our relationship with God and also with other members of the Body of Christ (*Catechism of the Catholic Church* [CCC], no. 1440). Take a moment to consider ways that you have broken any of the Ten Commandments: Are there any false "gods" (e.g., material things, pleasure, etc.) that you place above God and other people? Have you treated family members or others with disrespect? Have you lied, gossiped, cheated, or stolen?

## Sin is never an individual affair.

Sin damages our relationships with others and all of creation. Thus, sin is never a purely individual affair and has social dimensions (Pope Benedict XVI, *Sacramentum Caritatis* [*Sacrament of Charity*], no. 20; Pope John Paul II, *Reconciliatio et Paenitentia* [*Reconciliation and Penance*], no. 15).

## Sin becomes manifest in unjust structures.

The collective actions (or failures to act) of individuals create "structures of sin," which "grow stronger, spread, and become the source of other sins" (Pope John Paul II, *Sollicitudo Rei Socialis* [*On Social Concern*], no. 36). For example, widespread poverty, discrimination, denial of basic rights, and violence result from many peoples' actions (or failures to act) because of greed, racism, selfishness, or indifference (*Reconciliatio et Paenitentia*, nos. 2, 16). We are all called to consider how we contribute to structures of sin in our personal, economic, and public choices. For example, do we take into account the treatment of workers when we make purchases? How do our consumption choices contribute to environmental degradation? Are we aware and informed? Do we take the time to educate ourselves about issues that affect the community and advocate on behalf of those who are poor and vulnerable?

## We are called to examine our consciences and admit our failings.

The Sacrament of Penance challenges us to examine our hearts inwardly and then express outwardly the ways we have failed to love God and neighbor—through both personal sin and social sin.

Examining our consciences teaches us how to "look squarely at our life" to see how well we are living the Gospel (Pope Benedict XVI, Address to participants in the Course on the Internal Forum organized by the Tribunal of the Apostolic Penitentiary, March 25, 2011). Only in recognizing our failings can our hearts be converted to God so that we can receive his forgiveness and allow his grace to heal us and our relationships.

## We receive God's forgiveness and mercy.

The Sacrament of Penance allows us to receive forgiveness of sins and be reconciled with God, self, the Church family, and the human family—restoring our broken communion. Through Penance, we return to right relationships (*Sacramentum Caritatis*, no. 20).

## We work to repair the harm we have done.

Reconciliation absolves us of our sin, but it does not repair the damage that was caused. We must do what is possible to repair the harm. The *Catechism* provides these examples: return stolen goods, restore the reputation of someone slandered, and pay compensation for injuries (no. 1459). We must work to repair the relationships with God and our neighbors that sin has impaired. We must also consider how we can work to transform the structures of sin that threaten human life and dignity. By making amends and working to build a more just community, we can repair the damage and also restore our own spiritual health.

## The whole Church community plays a role in reconciliation.

We do not engage in the act of reconciliation alone. While the priest is the minister of the Sacrament of Penance, the whole Church community participates in the work of reconciliation (*Ordo Paenitentiae*). When we gather each Sunday, we call to mind our sins and intercede for one another. We hear the Word of God, which challenges us to reflect gospel values in our lives and relationships. As the Body of Christ, we also challenge one another to live lives of holiness, justice, and love. The Church is an instrument of conversion, calling all its members to love and reconciliation with God and neighbor.

## We are called to be forgivers and peacemakers.

Having received the undeserved gift of forgiveness, we are called to extend the same forgiveness and mercy to others. We take up the task of being instruments of reconciliation in our communities and world, working for peace, justice, and love.

## QUESTIONS FOR REFLECTION

Take a moment to reflect on how sin has damaged your relationship with others.

- What false "gods" do I place above God and people?
- After leaving Mass, do I continue to glorify God by the actions in my life?
- How have I failed to love others in my family, workplace, or community?
- Do I hold any views that are prejudiced or biased or that perpetuate stereotypes?
- Have I responded to the needs of the poor and those whose rights are unfulfilled?
- Do my personal, economic, and public choices reflect a genuine concern for others and the common good?
- Have I stood up to protect the dignity of others when it is being threatened?
- Am I aware of problems facing my local community and involved in efforts to find solutions?
- Do my purchasing choices take into account the well-being of those producing what I buy?
- How do I protect and care for God's creation? Are there ways I could reduce consumption?

Adapted from *Questions to Examine Conscience in the Light of Catholic Social Teaching* in the "Resources and Tools" section at *www.usccb.org/jphd*.

# Anointing of the Sick

## Joined to Christ, Witnesses of Hope and Healing

Anointing of the Sick is the sacrament that is received by those who are ill or suffering. By the sacred anointing and the prayer of the priest, the whole Church commends those who are sick to Christ. The sick person receives the Holy Spirit's gifts of strength, faith, peace, and courage, and his or her suffering is united with the suffering of Christ for the building up of the Church (*Catechism of the Catholic Church* [CCC], nos. 1520-23).

Through the Sacrament of Anointing of the Sick, the Church carries out Jesus' mission of compassion and healing for the sick. The one who is ill can also be a minister to others. By uniting their suffering to Christ, those who are sick can be signs of faith and witnesses of Christ's Resurrection to the entire community (Pope John Paul II, *Christifideles Laici* [*The Vocation and the Mission of the Lay Faithful in the Church and in the World*], no. 54).

## A Communal Celebration

The Sacrament of Anointing of the Sick is both "a liturgical and a communal celebration." In the family home, hospital, or church, members of the Body of Christ gather for the sacramental rite led by a priest. The Penitential Rite followed by the Liturgy of the Word and sacramental anointing of the sick can inspire and comfort both those who are ill and their family and friends who are gathered (CCC, nos. 1517-18). Many parishes have communal celebrations at which many persons receive the sacrament. These sacramental celebrations are a "source of strength amid pain and weakness, hope amid despair" and a "joyful encounter" for the entire community (*Christifideles Laici*, no. 54).

## Connection to the Communion of Saints

Anointing with sacred oil is a sign of blessing by the Holy Spirit of the one who is sick. Oil of the Sick, which receives a different blessing from the Chrism oil used during Baptism, Confirmation, and Holy Orders, recalls the community's sharing of the Holy Spirit and the sick person's connection to the entire Body of Christ and Communion of Saints.

## Imitation of Christ's Compassion

In the Gospels, Christ's great compassion toward the sick is expressed in the miraculous healings he performs, which heal the entire person, both body and soul. Parables such as the Good Samaritan (Lk 10:29-37) and

the Judgment of the Nations (Mt 25:31-46) urge Christ's followers to share his ministry of compassion and healing and to imitate his "preferential love for the sick" and all who suffer (CCC, nos. 1503, 1506; Pope Benedict XVI, *Sacramentum Caritatis* [*Sacrament of Charity*], no. 22).

## Solidarity with All Who Suffer

We care for the sick because we see them as children of God and part of our human family. When one part of the Body of Christ suffers, we all suffer (1 Cor 12:26). The suffering of one impacts everyone. Thus, we are called to solidarity, which is responsibility on the part of everyone with regard to everyone (Pope John Paul II, *Sollicitudo Rei Socialis* [*On Social Concern*], no. 38; Pope Benedict XVI, *Caritas in Veritate* [*Charity in Truth*], no. 38).

By our compassion, we remind those who are sick that "[the Church] shares your suffering. She takes it to the Lord, who in turn associates you with his redeeming Passion" (Synod of Bishops, *Per Concilii Semitas ad Populum Dei Nuntius*, no. 12). We are called to comfort, pray for and with, and be in solidarity with all who are sick or suffering.

Caring for those who suffer is not a burden, but a gift. Those who care for the sick do holy and important work; they walk with Christ's suffering people and in doing so, serve Christ himself (Mt 25:31-46). Those who minister to the sick and who work to secure decent health care for all become "the living sign of Jesus Christ and his Church in showing love towards the sick and suffering" (*Christifideles Laici*, no. 53).

### Union with Christ's Passion

While it is possible that the sacrament could bring physical healing, Anointing of the Sick is primarily about the healing of hope and of the spirit. Above all, the sacrament allows the person who is ill to unite more closely to Christ's Passion. This gives suffering a new meaning: a participation in the saving work of Jesus. This is a powerful witness that is for the good of the whole Church (CCC, nos. 1521-22).

### Beacons of Hope

Pope John Paul II wrote, "Even the sick are sent forth as laborers into the Lord's vineyard" (*Christifideles Laici*, no. 53). As the sick unite their sufferings to those of Christ, they become bearers of the joy of the Holy Spirit in the midst of affliction and witnesses of Christ's Resurrection. Anointing of the Sick testifies to the fact that all are called to participate in the redemption of the world (*Sacramentum Caritatis*, no. 22). We *all* have a role in sanctifying and building up the Church, whatever our physical condition. As the Synod of Bishops told an audience of sick and suffering persons, "We need you to teach the whole world what love is" (*Per Concilii Semitas ad Populum Dei Nuntius*, no. 12).

### A Witness to Dignity

The sacrament reminds us that each person is made in the image of God and has dignity that remains unchanged, whatever the body suffers. The ministry of those who are sick is a powerful witness to the fact that human dignity is intrinsic and does not increase or decrease based on a person's physical state or abilities. This is why the Church works to protect the life and dignity of the person at every stage of life—the embryo, the person suffering from AIDS, the family in poverty, and the person nearing death—and why she works to secure access to decent health care for all.

## QUESTIONS FOR REFLECTION

**For those who are ill:** Pope Paul VI, at the closing of the Second Vatican Council said:

> All of you who feel heavily the weight of the cross . . . you the unknown victims of suffering, take courage. You are the preferred children of the kingdom of God, the kingdom of hope, happiness and life. You are the brothers of the suffering Christ, and with Him, if you wish, you are saving the world. (Address to the poor, the sick, and the suffering)

*What role do you play in ministering to the People of God?*

**For those who are healthy:** Pope Benedict XVI noted:

> Following [Christ's] example, every Christian is called to relive, in different and ever new contexts, the Parable of the Good Samaritan who, passing by a man whom robbers had left half-dead by the roadside, "saw him and had compassion." (2010 Message for the World Day of the Sick)

*How are you called to follow Christ's example?*

Learn about the other sacraments! Visit "Resources and Tools" at **www.usccb.org/jphd**.

# Matrimony

## United in Love, Strengthened for Service

In Christian marriage, spouses model the love and self-gift of Christ. By giving of themselves and serving one another, their family, and community, they help one another live out Christ's call to discipleship, love, and service. Marriage provides a foundation for a family committed to community, solidarity, and Jesus' mission in the world.

### The love between spouses in marriage reflects the love of Christ for the Church.

The mutual love of spouses reflects God's own love for humanity (*Catechism of the Catholic Church* [CCC], no. 1604). In Scripture, God's "communion of love" with his people is seen in the covenant he forms with them, as well as in Jesus' self-offering on the Cross. The covenant of love into which spouses enter in marriage reflects the love of Christ for the Church and his self-gift on behalf of humanity (*Compendium of the Social Doctrine of the Church* [*Compendium*], no. 219).

### Marriage reflects the communion and union of the Trinity.

During the Rite of Marriage, the couple exchanges rings as a sign of love and fidelity in the name of the Father, Son, and Holy Spirit. Like the members of the Trinity, the united couple also becomes a "community of persons." Just as the Father, Son, and Spirit are united in "pure relationality," mutual love, and self-gift (Pope Benedict XVI, *Caritas in Veritate* [*Charity in Truth*], no. 54), Christian spouses are called to give of themselves to one another (Pope John Paul II, *Familiaris Consortio* [*On the Family*], no. 19).

### Marriage frees us for sacrifice and self-gift.

During the exchange of vows, the couple promises to give of themselves to each other and to love and support each other despite their shortcomings and failings. Spouses help each another "overcome self-absorption, egoism, [and] pursuit of one's own pleasure" so that they can serve others in imitation of Christ (CCC, no. 1609; *Compendium*, no. 219). With Christ's help, spouses are able to love, forgive, and serve (CCC, no. 1642). The Nuptial Blessing especially highlights how the couple is called to care not only for each another but also for children, family, and the wider community.

### Marriage strengthens us for service in the world.

The love between spouses helps them to be signs of Christ's love in the world (*Compendium*, no. 220). Their love for one another is realized in "the common work of watching over creation" (CCC, no. 1604). They help each other live their vocation as lay people, seeking God's Kingdom in their daily lives by working for justice, peace, and respect for the life and dignity of all (*Compendium*, no. 220; *Familiaris Consortio*, no. 47). Christian spouses, the *Compendium* notes, are to be "witnesses to a new social consciousness inspired by the Gospel and the Paschal Mystery" (no. 220).

## Marriage provides the foundation for family and the formation of "new citizens of human society."

From marriage comes the family, "in which new citizens of human society are born" and made children of God through the grace of the Holy Spirit in Baptism (*Lumen Gentium* [*Dogmatic Constitution on the Church*], no. 11). The home is called the "domestic church" (CCC, no. 1666)—the place where parents teach faith, love, justice, and concern for others to their children. Parents are "the principal and first educators of their children" (CCC, no. 1653). The family is the community where children "learn moral values, begin to honor God, and make good use of freedom" (CCC, no. 2207).

## The family gives testimony to faith, love, unity, peace, and justice.

The married couple—itself a sign of grace—works to form a family that is a "sign of unity for the world" and a "witness to the Kingdom" of justice and peace (*Compendium*, no. 220, *Familiaris Consortio*, no. 48). The home is the place where each person learns "solidarity and communal responsibilities" (CCC, no. 2224). Parents train children, from childhood on, to recognize God's love for all, to care for "their neighbors' needs, material and spiritual," to share in common with others, and to be involved in the local community (*Apostolicam Actuositatem* [*Decree on the Apostolate of Lay People*], no. 30).

## Marriage and the family inspire solidarity with the human family.

In the section called "The Family and Society," the *Catechism* notes that being a member of a family helps us to broaden our definition of who is included in our family. In our fellow citizens, we learn to see "the children of our country," in the baptized, "the children of our mother the Church," and in every human person, "a son or daughter" of the Father. Our relationships within the immediate family provide a foundation so that our relationships with all our neighbors become "personal." We come to recognize our neighbor not as a "unit" but as a "someone" who "deserves particular attention and respect" (no. 2212). In this way, the work for justice, life, and dignity begins in the family.

## The rights of families and married couples should be prioritized in public policy.

The well-being of individuals and societies is linked to "the healthy state of conjugal and family life" (*Gaudium et Spes* [*Pastoral Constitution on the Church in the Modern World*], no. 47). Therefore, we must "enact policies promoting the centrality and the integrity of the family founded on marriage between a man and a woman" and that "assume responsibility for [the family's] economic and fiscal needs" (*Caritas in Veritate*, no. 44).

In particular, we should preserve the rights of the family in civil laws and policies and work to ensure "that in social administration consideration is given to the requirements of families in the matter of housing, education of children, working conditions, social security and taxes" (*Apostolicam Actuositatem*, no. 11). We should also work to ensure that migrants' right to live together as a family is safeguarded.

## QUESTIONS FOR REFLECTION

- As a spouse or family member, how can you imitate the love of Christ and communion of the Holy Trinity in your own relationships?

- What can you do in your family to provide a strong foundation for faith, peace, solidarity with the global human family, and a commitment to the life and dignity of the human person?

# Holy Orders

## Ordained to Serve, Gather, Transform, and Send

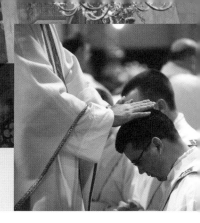

By virtue of our Baptism, all Christians are part of a *common priesthood* of believers. We are all called to participate in Christ's mission. Through the Sacrament of Holy Orders, bishops and priests are given a special role in carrying out this mission. They exercise a *ministerial priesthood*. Deacons also receive a special grace through ordination and are called to assist the ministry of bishops and priests (*Catechism of the Catholic Church* [CCC], nos. 1547, 1554).

Pope Benedict XVI writes, "The priest is above all a servant of others" (*Sacramentum Caritatis* [*Sacrament of Charity*], no. 23). In gathering the community, modeling Christ's love for the poor, presiding at Eucharist, and evangelizing social realities, ordained ministers help Christians imitate Christ's mission of love and justice.

### Representatives of Christ

Through ordination, priests become representatives of Christ to the Church—as witnesses of holiness and love, preachers of the Gospel, shepherds of the faithful, conveners of divine worship, and builders of the Church. Through their ministry, priests are called, in imitation of Christ, to "preach good news to the poor . . . proclaim release to the captives and recovery of sight to the blind, to set at liberty those who are oppressed, to proclaim the acceptable year of the Lord (Lk 4:18-19)" (Pope John Paul II, *Pastores Dabo Vobis* [*I Will Give You Shepherds*], no. 11). Deacons, too, are ordained to imitate Christ in his ministry of service and charity to the poor and needy in the community.

### Proclaimers of the Word

As co-workers with their bishops in teaching and carrying out Christ's mission, priests and deacons proclaim the Word of God to his people. This includes education about the social teaching of the Church, which is based in both Scripture and Tradition, and helping community members become aware of their "right and duty to be active subjects of this doctrine" (*Compendium of the Social Doctrine of the Church* [*Compendium*], no. 539).

### Pastors

Each bishop is entrusted with the care of a particular church, and priests and deacons assist in pastoring the people of God locally. Pastoral ministry requires that ordained ministers develop competency in "social analysis and community organization" and cross-cultural ministry (United States Conference of Catholic Bishops [USCCB], *The Basic Plan for the Ongoing Formation of Priests*, 29). Priests should "animate pastoral action in the social field," especially assisting lay Christians who are involved in political and social life (*Compendium*, no. 539). Pastoral concern extends beyond the local Church; bishops and priests must also attend to problems facing the people of the world, "sharing their experiences and growing, above all, in solidarity towards the poor" (Pope John Paul II, *Ecclesia in America* [*The Church in America*], no. 39)

### Presiders of Eucharist

Bishops and priests preside over the Eucharist, offering the sacrifice in the name of the whole Church, the Body of Christ (CCC, no. 1553). In celebrating the Eucharist, the Holy Spirit transforms the people of God for mission. In the words of Bishop William S. Skylstad:

> Especially at the celebration of Eucharist we help our people find Jesus in their lives through word, sacrament, and community. We also help them to appreciate that as they leave the church building they move into the world as eucharistic people. They too are to become "foot washers of humanity." (*Priests for a New Millennium*, 158).

In other words, through presiding over the Eucharist, priests help Christians to "live their social commitment" as a fruit of their worship (*Compendium*, no. 539).

## Builders of Community

Ordained ministry is a reminder of our "communitarian" nature, because it can only be carried out in communion with others. For example, priests minister in communion with their bishop, with other priests, and with the lay faithful. An important role of the priest is to bring together the entire community both in worship and in building the Church in the world. Being "a man of communion" means that a priest must be "a man of mission and dialogue," working for unity, justice, and peace with other faiths, people of good will, and with those who are poor and vulnerable (*Pastores Dabo Vobis*, nos. 17, 18).

## Missionaries

Pope John Paul II notes, "All priests must have the mind and the heart of missionaries," whether they serve near their home or across the world (*Redemptoris Missio* [*On the Permanent Validity of the Church's Missionary Mandate*], no. 67). Priests can have missionary hearts through their attentiveness to the struggles of their brothers and sisters across the world and by remembering "the whole Church for all of humanity" in their prayers and in the Eucharistic sacrifice (ibid.). This global perspective must be contagious;

priests must work to "form the community entrusted to them as a truly missionary community" (*Pastores Dabo Vobis*, no. 32). Deacons, too, have been sent by Christ and play an important role in bringing him to the heart of the parish community and beyond.

## Servants

St. John Vianney wrote, "The priesthood is the love of the heart of Jesus." Likewise, St. Augustine noted that the priesthood is the office of the good shepherd who offers his life for his sheep. In sum, "the priest is above all a servant of others" (*Sacramentum Caritatis*, no. 23). As Christ "emptied himself" (Phil 2:7) to become the suffering servant, so too, priests give themselves in service for the Church and the world. The celibate lifestyle, which encourages an undivided heart in those committed to it, fosters such self-emptying service. Deacons also exemplify service as they assist the bishop and priests in their ministries and dedicate themselves to ministries of charity (CCC, no. 1571).

## Advocates for the Poor

Ordained ministers are guided by the Holy Spirit to have "a preferential love for the poor, the sick, and the needy" and to identify with Christ the priest and victim (CCC, no. 1586). This special obligation to the poor and weak is in imitation of Jesus' own love for the poor and ministry to the sick and dying (*Presbyterorum Ordinis* [*Decree on the Ministry and Life of Priests*], no. 6).

## Counter-Witnesses

The ordained are to live in the world while also being witnesses representing virtues that lead the sheep to the one true sheepfold. These virtues include love, goodness, and "careful attention to justice" (*Presbyterorum Ordinis*, no. 3).

## Sharers of Catholic Social Teaching

Because the Church's social doctrine is an "essential component" of the "new evangelization" (*Pastores Dabo Vobis*, no. 54), those preparing for the ordained ministry should develop a "thorough knowledge" of Catholic social teaching and "a keen interest in the social issues of their day" (*Compendium*, no. 533).

## Evangelizers of Social Realities

Bishops, assisted by priests, deacons, and religious, must "evangelize social realities" (*Compendium*, no. 539) by being "articulate spokesmen for and interpreters of Catholic social teaching in today's circumstances" (USCCB, *Program of Priestly Formation*, no. 345).

# QUESTION FOR REFLECTION

How does this reflection help you to better understand the role of the bishop, priest, or deacon?

Learn about the other sacraments! Visit "Resources and Tools" at **www.usccb.org/jphd**.

# SESSION OUTLINE FOR SMALL GROUPS

**Session Length:** 75-90 minutes

## Materials Needed

- A Bible
- Copies of whichever sacrament handout is the topic of the session (one for each participant)
- Writing utensils (one for each participant)
- Loose leaf or note paper (Alternatively, you can provide, or ask participants beforehand to bring, a thin, three-ring binder for each participant with some blank paper inside, which can serve as a journal for recording their thoughts, reflections, and questions. If using this option, be sure to three-hole-punch the sacrament handouts so that participants can insert them in the binder.)

## Preparation

Arrange the chairs in a circle and set up a prayer space with an open Bible on a table in the center of the circle. Consider decorating the prayer space with a cloth, candle, small crucifix, or other items that do not obstruct the view of those around the circle when seated.

Open the Bible to the Scripture passage that corresponds to the theme of the session (see below).

Select one person ahead of time to read the passage at the appropriate time. Ask the person to read slowly and to return the Bible to the center table after reading.

## Introductions (10-20 minutes)

*Optional (additional 10 minutes):* Have "gathering" time for participants to get to know each other and form community. Provide "icebreaker" conversation topics for people to discuss in pairs as people are arriving, such as "What is your first memory of [insert name of sacrament]?" or "Why is [insert name of sacrament] meaningful to you?"

In the large group, each person should state his or her name and why he or she came.

## Opening Prayer (5 minutes)

The facilitator should remind everyone that the purpose of gathering today is to reflect on the Sacrament of [insert sacrament name] and the gospel call to mission.

Explain that the sacraments the Church celebrates are signs of grace that make a deeper reality present to us. One reality we encounter through the sacraments is Christ's presence in the Church community, his Body. This recognition of Christ's presence in the community should lead to a stronger awareness of being sent on mission to engage in concrete, love-inspired action in the world.

Invite everyone, in silence, to become aware of the presence of God.

Ask the first reader, selected before the session, to read the Scripture verse that corresponds to the topic of the session:

- **Baptism:** John 15:1-11 ("I am the vine, you are the branches")
- **Confirmation:** Luke 4:16-22 (Jesus proclaims, "The Spirit of the Lord is upon me . . .")
- **Eucharist:** John 6:1-15 (The multiplication of the loaves)
- **Penance and Reconciliation:** Matthew 25:31-36 (The sheep and the goats)
- **Anointing of the Sick:** Mark 2:1-12 (The healing of the paralytic)
- **Matrimony:** Matthew 5:13-16 (You are the light of the world) (Alternate possibility: Matthew 22:35-40 [The greatest Commandment])
- **Holy Orders:** John 21:15-17 ("Feed my lambs")

Pause for silent reflection on the Word of God for about 20 seconds.

Next, the leader should pray:

Loving Father,
Open our hearts to hidden realities:
  your love for all people,
  your presence in the community,
  your call to justice and peace.
May the sacraments stir in us
that same love for those with whom we worship
and all members of our human family.

Christ Jesus,
Help us to imitate your example:
  healing the sick,
  welcoming the stranger,
  assisting the poor and vulnerable.
May the sacraments remind us
of your love and self-giving,
which we strive to imitate.

Holy Spirit,
Make visible to our eyes what is invisible:
  your call to your people,
  your summons to live our faith daily
  as witnesses of justice and peace.
May the sacraments move us
to engage in love-inspired action
that transforms us and the world.

Amen.

## Sacrament Readings (15-20 min)

In the encyclical *Deus Caritas Est*, Pope Benedict XVI writes:

Jesus united into a single precept this commandment of love for God and the commandment of love for neighbor found in the Book of Leviticus: "You shall love your neighbor as yourself" (19:18; cf. Mk 12:29-31). Since God has first loved us (cf. 1 Jn 4:10), love is now no longer a mere "command"; it is the response to the gift of love with which God draws near to us. (no. 1)

Explain to participants that our call to love and care for our brothers and sisters is rooted first and foremost in God's love for us, which we learn and experience by imitating Jesus' own relationship with the Father. Our experience of God's love leads to our response. In today's session we will reflect on how our relationship with Christ, deepened through the sacraments, leads to loving response toward our neighbors in need.

Invite group members to take turns slowly reading paragraphs of the handout aloud.

Now invite group members to spend a few minutes re-reading the handouts on their own. The facilitator should give these instructions:

1. As you read, circle or underline the words or phrases that "jump out" at you.
2. When you are finished, go back to what you circled and make comments or notes in the margin, or on note paper, about why those words or phrases were meaningful.
3. *Optional (5-10 min): Ask participants to write down some thoughts or reactions on notepaper or in their journals.*

## Discussion (25-30 min)

Use the questions on the following page that correspond to the topic of the session. To help create a positive space for faith sharing, ask the participants to observe these simple guidelines:

- Listen carefully.
- Use "I" statements. (Take responsibility for what you express. Do not speak for "them.")
- Help all to participate. (Do not dominate.)
- Stay on the topic and stay focused on the pope's message.
- Be respectful and charitable at all times.
- Sharing that happens in the group should stay in the group.

## Discerning a Response (15 min)

Ask the participants:

- How has your perspective changed because of what we have discussed today? Do you see this sacrament differently?
- What concrete actions do you feel called to take in response?

Here are some questions the facilitator can ask to spark ideas about responses:

- Just as a cross has beams in two directions, vertical and horizontal, we are called to live our faith in two directions as well: vertical (our relationship with God) and horizontal (our relationship with others). Which is easier for you? Where do you need to grow?
- Which members of the communities you belong to are in need?
- What efforts are currently underway to ensure that the dignity of all is respected? How could you get involved?
- How are you, as a member of the Body of Christ, called to witness in the world, treasuring the life and dignity of each person?

## Closing Prayer (10 min)

Invite participants to offer spontaneous intercessions based on the session topic and discussion, praying "Lord, hear our prayer" after each intention. When everyone is finished offering intentions, end with the Lord's Prayer. Here are some sample intentions to use if needed.

### Baptism

For all who are part of the family of Christ, that awareness of our membership in the community will inspire us to care for all its members. We pray to the Lord . . .

For all new members, or soon-to-be-new members, of our Church through Baptism, including those whose names we mention now . . . (pause to allow names to be mentioned), that they may take up the baptismal call to discipleship. We pray to the Lord . . .

### Confirmation

For all who were recently confirmed, or who will be confirmed, including those whose names we mention now . . . (pause to allow names to be mentioned), that they may imitate the love and service of Christ and the saints. We pray to the Lord . . .

We pray in thanksgiving for the gifts of the Spirit in our own lives, especially those gifts we name now . . . (invite all to name a spiritual gift for which they are grateful), that we may use these gifts to serve the cause of justice and peace. We pray to the Lord . . .

### Eucharist

For all believers, that the Eucharist may challenge us to right relationship and solidarity with all who suffer. We pray to the Lord . . .

For those who are soon to make or who have recently made their First Communion, especially those who we now name . . . (pause to allow names to be mentioned), that they may live "Eucharistic" lives of service. We pray to the Lord . . .

### Penance and Reconciliation

For all sinners, that we may recognize the ways in which sin damages our relationships both with God and with others, prompting us to repentance and conversion. We pray to the Lord . . .

For our participation in structures of sin, especially those we mention now . . . (pause to allow examples to be mentioned), that the grace of the Holy Spirit may cleanse and purify us. We pray to the Lord . . .

### Anointing of the Sick

For the Church, that we may all imitate the compassion and love of Christ toward those who suffer. We pray to the Lord . . .

For all who are sick, especially those we mention now . . . (pause to allow names to be mentioned), that they may be witnesses of faith and hope. We pray to the Lord . . .

### Matrimony

For those who are engaged, especially those whose names we mention now . . . (pause to allow names to be mentioned), that their love for God and one another may strengthen them for service in the world. We pray to the Lord . . .

For all married couples, especially those whose names we mention now . . . (pause to allow names to be mentioned), that their marriages will provide a strong foundation for families committed to community, solidarity, and Christ's mission of love. We pray to the Lord . . .

### Holy Orders

For our bishop [insert name], our pastor [insert name], and for [insert names of other priests, and any deacons, who serve the parish], that through their ministry, they may serve as models of love and service, justice and peace. We pray to the Lord . . .

For those recently ordained or who are soon to be ordained, especially those we mention now . . . (pause to allow names to be mentioned), that they may carry out Christ's mission of charity and justice. We pray to the Lord . . .

# RESOURCES FOR FURTHER STUDY

Sacramental Catechesis: An Online Resource for Dioceses/Eparchies (SACCAT), Committee on Evangelization and Catechesis, United States Conference of Catholic Bishops (USCCB) (Fall 2012), **www.usccb.org/about/evangelization-and-catechesis**.

Electronic versions of the sacraments handouts are available in the "Resources and Tools" section of the USCCB Department of Justice, Peace and Human Development website at **www.usccb.org/jphd**.

# DISCUSSION QUESTIONS

## Baptism

"Baptism makes us members of the Body of Christ: 'Therefore . . . we are members one of another' (Eph 4:25)" (CCC, no. 1267).

Baptism is the rite of initiation into the Christian community. Through Baptism, we become members of the Body of Christ and are called to imitate Christ's mission.

1. What "jumped out at you" from the passages you read?
2. The Sacrament of Baptism is the rite of initiation into the Christian community. Why is community important to you? Why do you come here to worship instead of staying home to pray alone?
3. In what ways are the members of our faith community "connected to one another"? What do all people have in common as followers of Christ? How do our individual (and collective) actions (or inaction) affect one another?
4. Our Baptism makes us part of a "Communion of Saints," which strives to sacramentally make present the "Kingdom of God in history." What saints are you inspired by? How might you be called to imitate their example?
5. Baptism makes us participants in Christ's life and mission. In what ways are you called to "imitate" Christ and participate in his ministry of sacrifice, teaching, and love?
6. What is the connection between your Baptism and work to protect the life and dignity of every person?
7. *For parents*: How does faith and spiritual development relate to the lifelong nurturing of your child? Why is your child's journey of faith important to you?

## Confirmation

"By the sacrament of Confirmation, [the baptized] are more perfectly bound to the Church and are enriched with a special strength of the Holy Spirit" (CCC, no. 1285).

Confirmation enriches the baptized with the strength of the Holy Spirit so that they can better witness to Christ in word and deed (CCC, no. 1285). Anointed by the Holy Spirit at Confirmation, Christians strengthen their bond with the Church and become better equipped to carry out the Church's mission of love and service.

1. What "jumped out at you" from the passages you read?
2. What does it mean to be part of the Body of Christ? What benefits, and what responsibilities, does membership in this community entail?
3. At Confirmation, we are sealed with the gifts of the Holy Spirit. What do you see in yourself that the Spirit is calling out? How are you called to use those gifts to benefit others?
4. How do the lives of the saints inspire you to "give off the aroma of Christ"?
5. The Sacrament of Confirmation is an opportunity to reflect on the mission of love and service that God intends for each of our lives. How does what you have learned today help you inform your thinking about who are you called to be, what have you been called to do with your life, or what you feel you are called to do in the future?
6. What is the mission of the Church? What is your role in carrying it out? To what are you "com-missioned"?
7. The bishop (or his delegate) has "confirmed" your Baptism. How can you join your efforts to those of your bishop to participate in the Church's mission on behalf of those who are vulnerable?

## Eucharist

"The Eucharist commits us to the poor. To receive in truth the Body and Blood of Christ given up for us, we must recognize Christ in the poorest, his brethren" (CCC, no. 1397).

The Eucharist, celebrated as a community, teaches us about human dignity, calls us to right relationship with God, ourselves, and others, invites us to community and solidarity, and sends us on mission to help transform our communities, neighborhoods and world.

1. What "jumped out at you" from the passages you read?
2. Reflect on Blessed John Paul II's words: "A truly Eucharistic community cannot be closed in upon itself" (*Ecclesia de Eucharistia*, no. 39). Why is this the case?
3. How does the Eucharist challenge you to recognize your place within a community and the human family?
4. What kind of offering can you bring to the altar during the Eucharist?
5. Why and how must sharing in the sacrificial offering and reception of Holy Communion in the Eucharist sensitize us to those who suffer and move us to response?

6. What is the connection between Eucharist and mission? How is Eucharist connected to the call to respond to problems in your family, neighborhood, or community?

## Penance and Reconciliation

"Many sins wrong our neighbor. One must do what is possible in order to repair the harm. . . . Sin also injures and weakens the sinner himself, as well as his relationships with God and neighbor" (CCC, no. 1459).

Through the Sacrament of Penance, we are called to examine our consciences to identify those ways in which we are not in right relationship with God and with others. This examination also challenges us to recognize our own participation in the "structures of sin" that degrade others' lives and dignity, and to do what we can to repair the damage done.

1. What "jumped out at you" from the passages you read?
2. How are love of God and love of neighbor connected?
3. How is it true that sin is never an individual affair?
4. What are examples of "structures of sin" in our world? How do you personally contribute to them?
5. What actions might you be called to take to be a reconciler or peacemaker? To address social sin or lessen your involvement in it?

## Anointing of the Sick

"Christ invites his disciples to follow him by taking up their cross in their turn. By following him they acquire a new outlook on illness and the sick. Jesus associates them with his own life of poverty and service. He makes them share in his ministry of compassion and healing" (CCC, no. 1506).

Through the Sacrament of Anointing of the Sick, the Church carries out Jesus' mission of compassion and healing for the sick. The one who is ill can also be a minister to others. By uniting their suffering to Christ, those who are sick can be signs of faith and witnesses of Christ's Resurrection to the entire community.

1. What "jumped out at you" from the passages you read?
2. How does this sacrament emphasize the community of the Church as the "Body of Christ"?
3. The person who is ill and the ones who are healthy both "minister" to one another through this sacrament in different ways. What is the role of each? Why are both important?
4. How is this sacrament a reflection of the ministry of Christ?
5. How can a person who is sick act as a beacon of hope for others?
6. How can our presence to and advocacy for those who are sick transform us and others?

## Matrimony

"[A man and woman's] mutual love becomes an image of the absolute and unfailing love with which God loves man. It is good, very good, in the Creator's eyes. And this love which God blesses is intended to be fruitful and to be realized in the common work of watching over creation" (CCC, no. 1604).

In Christian marriage, spouses model the love and self-giving of Christ. By giving of themselves and serving one another, their family, and community, they help one another live out Christ's call to discipleship, love, and service. Marriage provides a foundation for a family committed to community, solidarity, and Jesus' mission in the world.

1. What "jumped out at you" from the passages you read?
2. What is the relationship between the love of Christ for the Church and the love between spouses in marriage? How have you seen this in your own relationship or that of others?
3. How does marriage strengthen us for service to both God and the human family?
4. What is the relationship between loving your spouse and loving others?
5. As a spouse or family member, how can you imitate the love of Christ and communion of the Holy Trinity in your own relationships?
6. What can you do in your family to provide a strong foundation for faith, peace, solidarity with the global human family, and commitment to the life and dignity of every human person?
7. What can society and/or public policy do to better encourage healthy marriages and families?

## Holy Orders

"This sacrament configures the recipient to Christ by a special grace of the Holy Spirit, so that he may serve as Christ's instrument for his Church" (CCC, no. 1581).

In gathering the community, modeling Christ's love for the poor, presiding at Eucharist, and evangelizing social realities, ordained ministers help Christians imitate Christ's mission of love and justice.

1. What "jumped out at you" from the passages you read?
2. How does this reflection help you better understand the role of the bishop, priest, or deacon?
3. What does the ordained's role to sanctify and bless say about God's creation as a gift for us to protect and use responsibly?
4. How are the ordained called to be "above all a servant of others"?
5. What is the role of the deacon, priest, and bishop in "evangelizing social realities"? How can they do this?
6. How are the members of the "common priesthood of believers" and those ordained into the "ministerial priesthood" called to work together to address poverty and injustice?